ROAD TRIP

APRIL FOOLS!

WHOA! I JUST THOUGHT OF SOMETHING...WE OUGHTA GO ON "BODS"!

YEAH ≥HEH-HEH≤ BUT NOT JUST ANYONE'S BODS...WE SHOULD GO ON SOME GIRLS' BODS, ≥HEH-HEH≤

WE SHOULD GO ON THE SHOW "BODS", DUMBASS.

BODS TV

AUDIENCE ENTER HERE

CONTESTANTS ENTRANCE

THIS IS GONNA BE COOL! NOW CHICKS'LL HAFTA DATE US!

OH YEAH ≥HEH-HEH≤

BACKSTAGE.

HI, I'M THE PRODUCER OF "BODS"! WELCOME TO OUR CONTESTANT TRYOUT. NOW IF YOU GUYS ARE ANY-THING LIKE THE TYPICAL VIEWERS OF OUR SHOW, YOU'RE SEXIST MALE-CHAUVINIST PIGS.

UH ≥HUH-HUH≤ THAT'S US, MA'AM.

YEAH ≥HEH-HEH≤ OINK!! OINK!

LIKE, WHAT'S YOUR SIGN OR SOMETHING?

DEATH ROCK

SHOW 3
JIM
ARCHIE
STAN
ROY

...LOOK...

LET'S GET ONE THING STRAIGHT...

...YOU'RE WELCOME TO BE YOUR USUAL, UNPLEASANT SELVES WHEN AND IF I EVER LET YOU ON THE SHOW... BUT DON'T ACT LIKE JERKS AROUND ME! IF I EVER LET

BODS

≥HUH-HUH≤ SHE SAID, "GET ONE THING STRAIGHT"

YEAH. ≥HEH-HEH≤ AN' I THINK IT WORKED!

PART 2 "SHE'S MY DATE, DUMBASS!"

COOL! WE'RE GONNA, LIKE, CALL CHICKS AN' ASK 'EM OUT, AN' SCORE!

YEAH! THIS RULES!

DEATH ROCK

... MOST CHICKS TELL ME THAT THEY, LIKE, DON'T HAVE A PHONE, AN' STUFF...

CHECK OUT THESE STATISTICS, DUDE...

...36-24-35!

"BODS"
CONTESTANT FACT SHEET

NAME: CRYSTAL L. BALL
AGE: 18 HT: 5'4" WT: 103
OCCUPATION: ACTRESS
HOBBIES: READING, DANCING
MEASUREMENTS: 36-24-35

WHOA!

...I DIDN'T KNOW I.Q.s WENT THAT HIGH.

UH, YOURS SURE DOESN'T, BEAVIS...

OH YEAH.

UH, I'LL CALL AND ASK FOR THE FIRST DATE, DUDE...

NO WAY! LET ME CALL FIRST, FARTKNOCKER!! I'VE HAD MORE PRACTICE! ...CALLING 900 NUMBERS AND STUFF...

LEGGO, DUMBASS! YOU'RE GETTING ON MY NERVES!

NO WAY! I WANNA JUMP ON SOME CHICK'S NERVES, OR SOMETHING.

HELLO...

UH... HEY BABY! HOW 'BOUT A DATE?

YEAH! ME, TOO!

LATER...

AS SOON AS SHE SHOWS UP, YOU GOTTA GET **LOST**, DUDE.

OKAY, UHM, ME AND HER ARE GONNA GET LOST **TOGETHER**, AND **YOU** BETTER NOT TRY AND **FIND** US, FARTKNOCKER.

PLAYING "BASEBALL" WITH A CHICK IS GONNA BE COOL! I MIGHT GET MY **BATTER UP**, AND THEN **SCORE** WITH A HOME RUN...OR AT LEAST GET "ON BASE"! ₹ HUH-HUH ₹

YEAH! AN' THEN LATER **I'LL** TRY AN' HAVE SEX WITH HER! ₹ HEH-HEH ₹

UH, DON'T GET YOUR **HOPES** UP, DUDE. YOUR LIFETIME BATTING AVERAGE WITH CHICKS IS .000. ₹HUH-HUH ₹

UHM... DO YOU THINK I'M HOLDING MY **BAT** WRONG?

NO, I THINK YOU'RE HOLDING IT TOO **MUCH!** ₹ HUH-HUH ₹

OH, YEAH. ₹ HEH-HEH ₹

HERE SHE COMES, DUDE... WITH HER "BASES" LOADED! ₹HUH-HUH ₹

GET LOST, KIDS...I'M MEETING A **DATE** HERE.

UH...PLEASED TO MEET YOU...

ME, TOO. PLEASE, MEET ME!

I HAVE A DATE WITH **YOU** TWERPS? **BOTH** OF YOU?!

UH... BEAVIS IS JUST TAGGING ALONG...

BUTT-HEAD'S TAGGING ALONG, TOO... ...IT'S, LIKE, A **DOUBLE DATE!**

UH...I BET **EVERY** DATE YOU GO ON IS, LIKE, A **DOUBLE DATE**, OR SOMETHING. ₹ HUH-HUH ₹...

YEAH! ₹ HEH-HEH-HEH ₹

LATER THAT NIGHT...

ARE YOU READY FOR, UH, "BACHELORETTE NUMBER THREE, DUDE?

YEAH! HEH-HEH! MADAME PALM RULES!

NO, THAT'S "BACHELORETTE NUMBER FOUR"-- YOU'LL BE MEETING HER ALONE.

QUICK--! GET IN THE CAR!

WHOA! SHE WANTS IT!!

...BEFORE ANYONE SEES ME TALKING TO YOU LOSERS!!!

UH... COOL MOVIE... HOW ABOUT A KISS...?

NO WAY, FARTKNOCKER!

I WAS TALKING TO HER!

NO WAY, FARTKNOCKER.

UH, MAYBE SHE'S ONE OF THOSE CHICKS THAT DOESN'T ENJOY MAKING OUT, OR DOING IT, OR ANYTHING.

OH, YEAH. I MEET LOTSA CHICKS LIKE THAT.

SHORTLY...

HI! I'M COURTNEY...

MIND IF I BORROW YOUR DATE, TWERPS?

UH, YOU CAN HAVE HER AS SOON AS WE'RE DONE WITH HER, DUDE.

THAT'S NO WAY TO TALK AROUND A LADY...

...ESPECIALLY A LADY THAT'S GONNA SCORE WITH ME!!

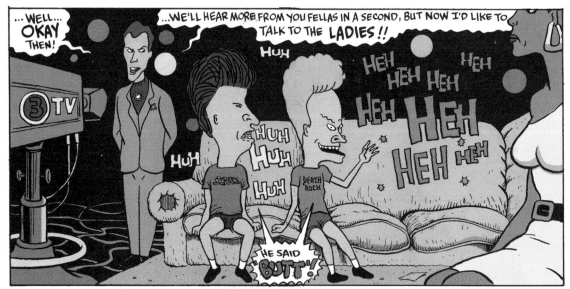

TELL US HOW **YOUR** TWO DATES WENT, CRYSTAL!

ACTUALLY, IT WAS JUST **ONE** DATE... I SAW BOTH OF THEM AT THE SAME TIME...

...WHICH WAS FANTASTIC...

YOU MEAN BECAUSE YOU WERE ABLE TO, UH, "**DOUBLE** YOUR PLEASURE"?

YES!

OH, YEAH. ¿HEH-HEH? WE'RE PRETTY COOL.

SEE HAZ-MZ-H GLENN

DEATH ROCK

NO... I MEAN BECAUSE I ONLY HAD TO WASTE **ONE** AFTERNOON WITH THOSE LOSERS...

...THEY'RE A COUPLE OF DISGUSTING PATHETIC **CREEPS.**

...I MEAN, THEY'RE **CRUEL** TO **ANIMALS!!!**

NOTE: IVORY EARRINGS!

...ONE OF THEM ACTUALLY TALKED ABOUT SOME POOR **MONKEY** THAT HE SPANKED!

SKULL

...AND THEY'RE SO **DUMB!**

...OH, YEAH. WE'RE PRETTY COOL...

SHUT **UP** DUMBASS!

...WOULD YOU CARE TO TELL US **YOUR** VERSION OF WHAT HAPPENED ON THAT DATE...?

I'M NOT TH' KISS AN' TELL **TYPE,** DUDE.

SKULL

¿HEH-HEH? WE'RE GONNA PLAY SHOW AN' TELL—— **COOL!**

UHM... LEMME GO FIRST! I'LL **TELL** YOU CHICKS WHAT TO **SHOW** ME...

¿HEH-HEH-HEH?

...YOU CAN **START** WITH YOUR "THINGIES"

SIGH! **GASP! SHOCK! GULP! FAINT! REACT!**

UH, HUH-HUH! YOU'RE PRETTY COOL, BEAVIS.

YOUR TURN, JASMYN!

WHAT SEXY DATING STORY CAN YOU TELL US?

TO BE HONEST WITH YOU, I WOULDN'T CALL MEETING TWO GUYS OUTSIDE A SEEDY MOTEL AND THEN BEING INVITED TO "PICNIC" OUT OF A DUMPSTER A DATE!

NEITHER WOULD I...

...BUT I DO THINK IT COULD BE KIND'A KINKY...

...THINK AGAIN.

UH, OKAY, THEN! COURTNEY!! HOW DID YOUR DATE GO?

WELL...THE EVENING BEGAN WITH A DRIVE-IN MOVIE...

WHOO-EE! THAT'S ALWAYS A GOOD START FOR A DATE!

YEAH! MOVIES ARE PRETTY COOL!

I DIDN'T CARE MUCH FOR THE MOVIE...

...BUT...

...THE SEX AFTERWARD WAS TERRIFIC!

...NOW WE'RE GETTIN' SOMEWHERE! TELL ME MORE!

UH... =HUH-HUH=... ..THERE WAS SEX?

UHM... I DON'T REMEMBER THAT PART...

THIS IS STARTING TO SUCK!

YEAH! WHEN DO WE SCORE?

UH, MAYBE LATER, GUYS...

RIGHT NOW IT'S TIME TO SEE HOW WELL YOU GOT TO KNOW THESE FABULOUS BABES!

... I'LL READ THREE QUOTES, AND YOU SEE IF YOU CAN TELL WHO SAID WHAT...

"...THEY MADE WAVES OF PLEASURE RIPPLE THROUGH MY BODY... JUST BY ENDING THE DATE."

"... NOTHING HAS EVER GIVEN ME MORE SHEER JOY THAN WATCHING MY NEW BOYFRIEND TODD BEAT THEM UP."

"...THEY'RE BOTH TOTAL LOSERS..."

"... EVEN SECOND BASE WAS TOTALLY OUT OF THE QUESTION."

UH... HUH-HUH; NONE OF THE ABOVE?

HEH-HEH; CAN YOU REPEAT THE QUESTION?

SORRY GUYS, WE'RE ALMOST AT THE END OF OUR SHOW. NOW'S THE TIME WHEN WE ASK EACH CONTESTANT IF THEY'D LIKE TO MEET AGAIN.

UH, I'D LIKE TO SEE ALL OF 'EM AGAIN.

ME, TOO. ALL SIX OF 'EM, HEH-HEH;

NEVER!!!

WELL, THAT'S "BODS" FOR TODAY.

THANKS FOR WATCHING THE SHOW THAT ASKS "ARE YOU GETTIN' ANY?"

...WELL, ARE WE?

UH, NO. YOU BOYS PROBABLY NEVER WILL. BUT WE DO HAVE A CONSOLATION PRIZE FOR YOU GUYS...

... IT'S THE HOME VERSION OF "BODS"!

LATER...

SO, UH, DID YOU, HUH-HUH; "DO IT"?

UHM, DO WHAT?

YOU DUMBASS.

OH, YEAH, "IT"!

DON'T WORRY.

I "DID IT"!

I FLUSHED. HEH-HEH;

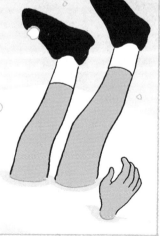

SOON...

WONDERFUL!

WUP WUP WUP WUP WUP WUP WUP WUP

YES!!!

YEAH! HELICOPTERS ARE COOL!

UHM, I WONDER WHERE IT'S HEADED?

BOY! ARE WE GLAD TO SEE YOU!

YEAH-HUH= YOU'RE THE FIRST CHICK WE'VE SEEN ALL DAY!

NOT COUNTING CHICKS ON TV, OR THE SNOW-CHICK ME AND BUTT-HEAD MADE.

WE HEARD YOUR PECULIAR DISTRESS CALL AND CAME RIGHT AWAY!

YOUR SPEED IN HELP-ING OTHERS IS TRULY INSPIRING.

WELL, WE WERE AFRAID IF THAT MORON KEPT SHOUTING, HE'D TRIGGER AN AVALANCHE THAT WOULD DESTROY OUR RESCUE STATION.

OH, YEAH. SHOUTING'S COOL! IT RULES! IT RULES!!

IT RULES!

SHUT UP!

...NOW DOES ANYONE REQUIRE IMMEDIATE MEDICAL ATTENTION?

UH, BEAVIS THINKS HE HAS FROSTBITE IN HIS =HUH-HUH= "EXTREMITY"

I'D BETTER TAKE A LOOK AT THAT, YOUNG MAN.

EH=HEH-HEH= IT SEEMS TO BE GOING AWAY NOW.

THANK YOU FOR YOUR CONCERN!

UH...YOU CAN LOOK AT MY "EXTREMITY" IF YOU WANT...

OH YEAH! =HEH-HEH= ME, TOO!

...THEN YOU COULD DO IT WITH US! =HUH-HUH-HUH=

YEAH! =HEH-HEH= THAT'D BE PRETTY COOL!

IF YOU TWO DON'T SHUT UP, YOU WON'T BE GETTING OFF THIS MOUNTAIN!!!

ANGELA

EH= HEH-HEH= OKAY, SINCE WE'RE GONNA BE STUCK HERE AWHILE, WHY DON'T YOU LIKE, SHOW US YOUR OWN MOUNTAINS, OR SOMETHING.

=HUH-HUH= SHE SAID "GETTING OFF"!

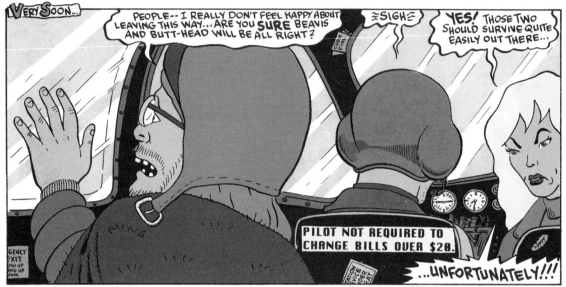

VERY SOON...

PEOPLE-- I REALLY DON'T FEEL HAPPY ABOUT LEAVING THIS WAY... ARE YOU **SURE** BEAVIS AND BUTT-HEAD WILL BE ALL RIGHT?

≈SIGH≈

YES! THOSE TWO SHOULD SURVIVE QUITE EASILY OUT THERE...

PILOT NOT REQUIRED TO CHANGE BILLS OVER $20.

...UNFORTUNATELY!!!

BUT... BUT... ...I CAN HARDLY EVEN **SEE** THEM DOWN THERE.

WUP WUP WUP WUP

...THIS ISN'T RIGHT.

PLEASE TRY AND **RELAX**, SIR! YOU'VE JUST BEEN THROUGH A VERY **STRESSFUL** SITUATION.

...AFTER ALL, YOU DID SPEND SEVERAL **HOURS** ALONE WITH THOSE TWO MORONS.

I GUESS YOU'RE RIGHT...

...IT **IS** A RELIEF NOT TO HAVE THEM HERE IN THE CABIN...

THAT'S THE SPIRIT, SIR! I'LL TELL THE PILOT TO SPEED UP...

HUH-HUH-HUH-H   HUH-HUH-HU

RESCUE

HEH-HEH-HEH-HEH

...MAYBE THE SOUND OF THE ENGINE WILL DROWN OUT THAT INFERNAL **LAUGHTER.**

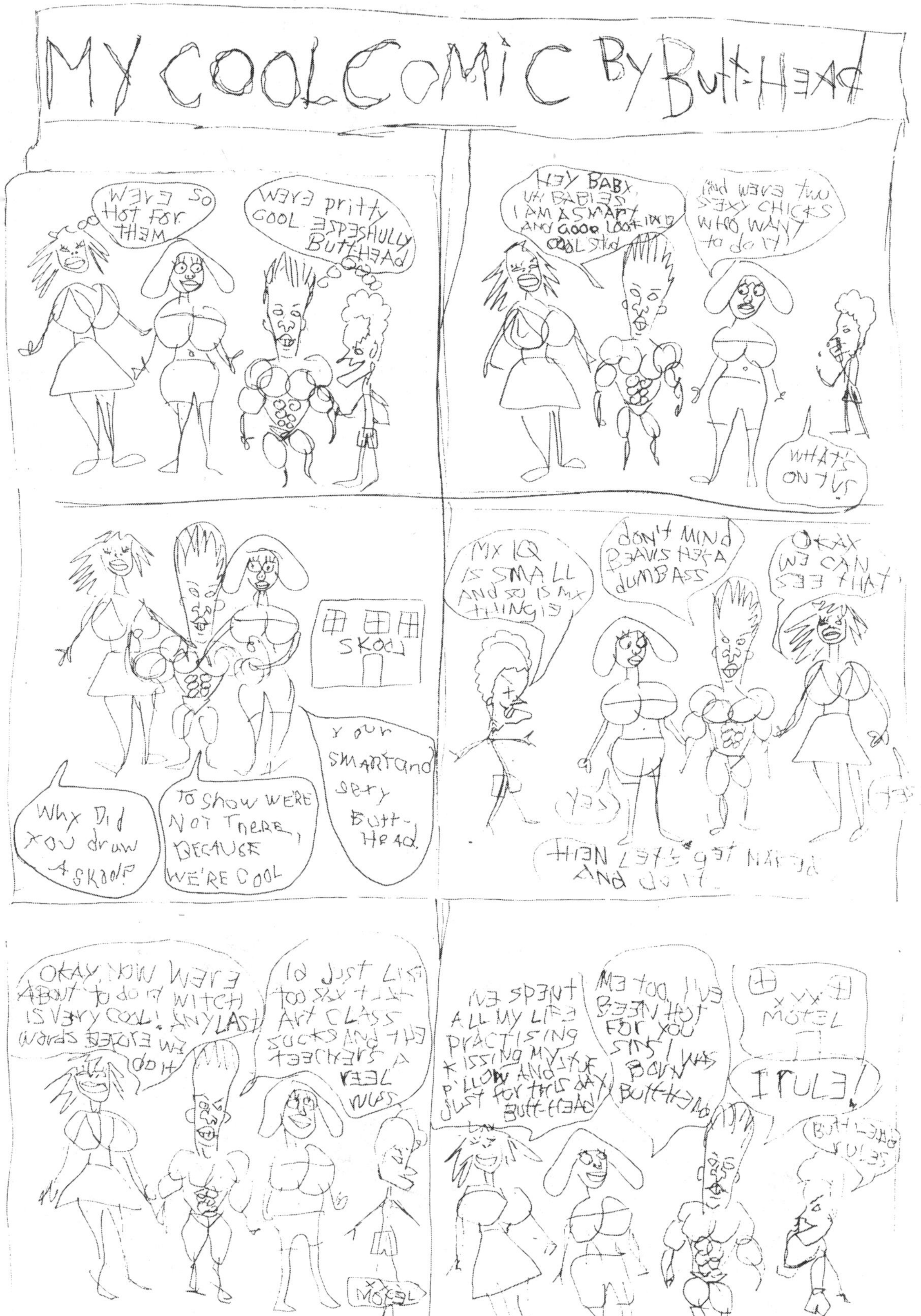

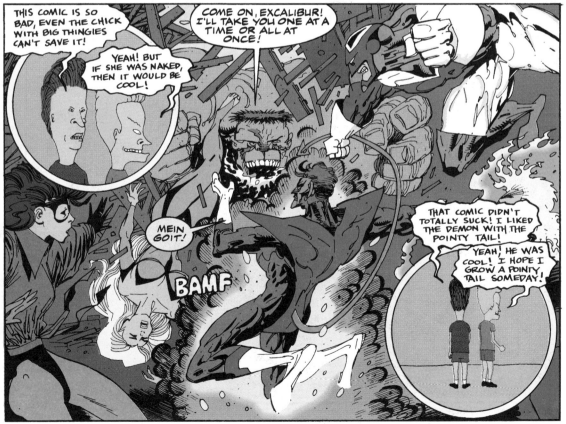

BEAVIS AND BUTT-HEAD DIALOGUE BY TOM FIELD.
CYCLOPS & PHOENIX ART & WORDS BY GENE HA. AND ART LYON.

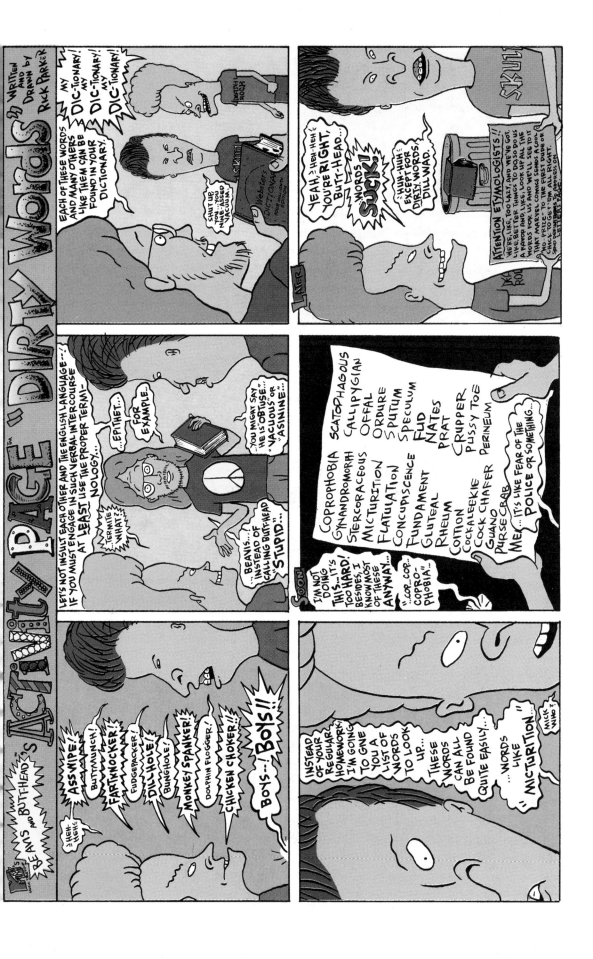

OUR "APRIL FOOL'S DAY" TRADITION DATES BACK CENTURIES AND IS SHARED BY MANY CULTURES. WHEREAS WE AMERICANS LIKE TO SHOUT "APRIL FOOLS!" AT THE VICTIMS OF OUR PRACTICAL JOKES ON THIS DAY, THE FRENCH LIKE TO SHOUT "POISSON D'AVRIL!" OR "APRIL FISH!"

YES, BUTT-HEAD--? DO YOU HAVE A QUESTION?

YEAH... MY QUESTION IS: WHO GIVES A RAT'S ASS?

THAT KIND OF LANGUAGE ISN'T VERY PRO-ACTIVE, BUTT-HEAD...

...UH, DID I USE LANGUAGE?

HEH-HEH-MM-HEH... YOU SAID "ASS" IN CLASS!

OH, YEAH! SO, LIKE "APRIL FOOLS!" OR SOMETHING. HUH-HUH-HUH

HMMM... THAT'S AN UNUSUAL APRIL FOOL'S JOKE, I MUST SAY... BUT IN THE SPIRIT OF THE DAY, I THINK I'LL ALLOW IT, BUTT-HEAD...

...CLASS DISMISSED...

ITCH ITCH

THAT WAS PRETTY COOL!

YOU MEAN WHEN YOU SAID "ASS"?

HEH-HEH-MM-HEH... "ASS" IN CLASS. NOW I SAID IT HEH-HEH.

ARE YOU VOTING?

DID YOU FILL YOURS OUT YET?

UH, THAT WAS COOL, TOO, DUDE. BUT THE REALLY COOL PART WAS WHEN VAN DRIESSEN LET ME SAY IT, 'CAUSE IT WAS, LIKE "APRIL FOOLS", OR WHATEVER.

OH YEAH! BEING FOOLS RULES!!

IT'S LIKE, YOU CAN DO WHATEVER YOU WANT AND THEN JUST SAY "APRIL FOOLS."

CHECK THIS OUT...

UH...HEY BABY!! WANNA "DO IT"? HUH-HUH-HUH

LET'S PUT IT THIS WAY: IF YOU WERE THE LAST BOY ON EARTH, AND IF I WAS THE LAST GIRL, AND IF GETTING INTIMATE WITH YOU WAS THE ONLY WAY TO SAVE HUMANITY FROM TOTAL EXTINCTION...

YEAH?

...I STILL WOULDN'T EVEN CONSIDER IT....

WELL...UH...= HUH-HUH APRIL FOOLS!!

IT WAS, LIKE A TRICK QUESTION OR SOMETHING.

WHOA! YOU'RE PRETTY COOL, BUTT-HEAD.

MTV's BEAVIS AND BUTT-HEAD IN: SPIN THE BOTTLE

GUY MAXTONE-GRAHAM ... WRITER
RICK PARKER ARTIST
ROB CAMACHO COLOR
GLENN HERDLING EDITOR
CARL POTTS EDITOR IN CH
GLENN EICHLER CONSUL
MIKE JUDGE CREATOR

THE PRINCIPAL'S OFFICE IS COOL!

YEAH, HUH-HUH! LET'S GET SENT THERE AGAIN NEXT TIME THERE'S A TEST!

WE'RE THERE, DUDE.

OKAY!! LISTEN UP, EVERYBODY!! THERE'S GONNA BE A PARTY AT MY HOUSE STARTING AT 8:00 TONIGHT! I REALLY HOPE YOU'LL ALL SHOW UP...AND BRING ANYONE ELSE YOU WANT!

I will not write dirt stuff on the blac
I will not write d stuff on the blo
I will not write stuff on the blac

NOW, KIMBERLY...ISN'T THERE SOMETHING YOU'D LIKE TO TELL BEAVIS AND BUTT-HEAD ABOUT?

C'MON... YOU REALLY SHOULD TELL THEM ABOUT WHAT THEY MISSED OUT ON WHILE THEY WERE RAPPING WITH PRINCIPAL McVICKER...

UH... IF IT'S LIKE HOME-WORK OR SOMETHING I DON'T WANNA HEAR ABOUT IT.

YEAH, ME TOO.

KIMBERLY, YOU CAN'T INVITE THE ENTIRE CLASS EXCEPT FOR TWO PEOPLE.

THERE'S A PARTY AT MY HOUSE TONIGHT. IF YOU TWO INSIST ON COMING, FEEL FREE TO SHOW UP REALLY LATE AND THEN LEAVE REALLY EARLY. AND IF YOU'D RATHER STAY HOME OR CRAWL UNDER A ROCK SOMEWHERE, INSTEAD OF SHOWING YOUR FACES AT MY PARTY, THAT WOULD BE PERFECTLY FINE.

COOL!

SHE WANTS US, DUDE.

WE'RE GONNA SCORE!

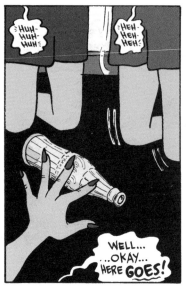

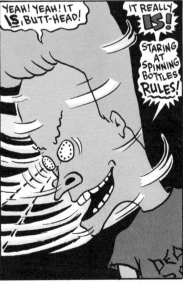

FUN ART

FUN WITH ANIMALS

NATIVE AMERICAN
HUMOR
(BEAVIS AND BUTT-HEAD STYLE)